On the Other Side of a Heart Attack

Poems by Terry Loncaric

Illustration by Julie Vander Meulen

ISBN: 978-93-6354-515-1

First Edition: 2025
Rs. 200/-

Cyberwit.net
HIG 45 Kaushambi Kunj, Kalindipuram
Allahabad - 211011 (U.P.) India
http://www.cyberwit.net
Tel: +(91) 9415091004
E-mail: info@cyberwit.net

Printed at Repro India Limited.

Devoted to all heart attack survivors. May we become thrivers in spite of our setbacks. Devoted to the doctors, nurses, paramedics, therapists, and other health care professionals, who work so hard to mend our hearts and heal us. In our moment of crisis, may we always remember to feel gratitude for the blessings that empower us to keep living.

Heart disease is the No. 1 killer of men and women worldwide. The warning signs can be especially subtle for women and can often be mistaken for other illnesses. Warning signs for women may include jaw pain, dizziness, insomnia, anxiety, indigestion, and nausea. Fatigue and being short-of-breath are common symptoms for both sexes. When in doubt, it is always wise to consult with a doctor.

Contents

The Heart Attack

A herd of elephants stampeded, then sat on my chest.
I will do anything to get out of a bad movie.
The ambulance ride, a blur.
I was riding high an adrenaline, as I often do,
in a crisis situation, my humor, a total mask
for the fact I was scared shitless.
Is this a cruel joke, I had a heart attack
just days before American Heart Month,
right before seeing Amy Grant admit on TV
she had some hidden heart problem?
Grief came crashing at my door, the realization
that a major organ had failed me, or maybe I failed it.
The Bible says, the body is a temple.
Is it possible mine had become a New Orleans street fair?
So much to process, in so little time,
a raft of new meds, a radical change in eating habits,
the letting go of my delusions, stripped naked,
forced to admit, I am not, and never was, invincible.
I didn't need Amy Grant to tell me that.
I knew it, God knew it, the heart doctor knew it.
A moment of complete darkness, total surrender,
a punch in the gut, the stark realization, I could have died.
I never will be the same, I am now a heart attack survivor.
A chance for redemption, a time for transformation.
I made it out alive, I am not helpless.
I am, as one friend described it, living my second life.
Maybe it is my best life. I sure as hell hope so.

So Random

Luck changes its meaning
when you have a close brush
with death.
Luck is having a heart attack
in a movie theater, only
five minutes from a hospital.
Luck is having a heart attack
and not being alone.
Luck is having a heart attack
right before your two
99 percent blocked arteries
become 100 percent blocked.
Luck is so random.

Ticking Bomb

It never
dawned on me
I was a ticking
time bomb.
I loved to eat.
I hated to work out.
What was I thinking?

Nurse Brittany

I didn’t even know your last name,
yet we shared a precious moment,
an intimate moment,
in a dimly lit hospital room,
just before the news bulletin,
a plane and helicopter crashed, then plunged
into the icy waters of the Potomac.
You arrived at just the right moment
to witness my tears, my fears,
to talk about the baby
who was soon to exit your belly.
Do you have any idea how reassuring
it felt to hear about new life —
when my life almost ended,
after the boulder landed on my chest,
after the baby aspirin,
after the nitroglycerine,
after the blare of ambulance sirens?
The reality sank in,
I really did have a heart attack.
I lived to tell the tale,
and you, a compassionate stranger,
bore witness to the crash of my vulnerability.

Most Excellent Adventure

I always thought
it would be an adventure
to stay in a hospital,
to be pampered 24/7,
to have breakfast in bed.
What was I thinking?
Awakened constantly
by a parade of people
monitoring, probing,
sticking and bruising.
On the other hand,
getting waited on
around the clock
was not so bad.
The hospital food?
Not so much.

Determined

Some people say
I am brave.
Not really.
I survived.
Like my astrological
sign, the goat,
I am too stubborn
to do anything else.
I have become
an active agent
of my own health.
The will to live
is wicked strong.
Nothing is quite
as motivating
as the possibility
of death.
Too many poems,
too many
nature walks,
too many
life experiences
still left in my
ever-changing
bag of tricks.
I am anchored
in the belief,
the will to survive
will always defeat

the desire to slide
into lazy choices.
Failure is not
an option.
You could say
a heart attack
saved my life.
Brave?
Not so much.
Determined
to stay alive.
Glad to be here.
Eager to
to free-fall
into the next
adventure
without fear
or trepidation.
Intensely grateful.

The Other Side

Don't ask me how
or even why.
I just know it was not
my day to disappear.
An unseen force to guide me,
a feeling I could walk
with great clarity
and utter gentleness
to the other side,
not slip into the abyss.
Maybe it was the love
of a mother and father,
who taught me survival skills.
Maybe it was sheer tenacity.
All I knew is I could make it
to the other side of my heart failure,
as if I was traveling to a place
I was meant to visit,
to feel the lightness of this life,
and what I have yet
to accomplish.

Minimizer No More!

I dismissed.
I discounted.
I minimized.
That's what women do.
It is our way of avoiding
unpleasant situations
we have been conditioned
to believe we can't handle.
I could explain away
the tightness in the chest.
It was indigestion.
I could justify my
shortness of breath.
I am out of shape,
and I was climbing
a steep flight of stairs.
Why wouldn't I feel dizzy?
I was running around
doing too many errands
on a muggy summer day.
In all of these situations,
I failed to connect the dots,
or I was not willing
to take the time
to simply listen to my body.
Why borrow problems?
The cup is always half-full,
isn't it?

It couldn't be anything serious,
could it???
Looking back, I realize
I should have recognized
the red lights that were
flashing so clearly in my eyes.
Minimizing was my
twisted way of coping.
How else could I rake
through the complex layers
of a hectic life?
For way too long,
I was good at avoidance.
Now I am vigilant,
too smart to ignore my body
when it is sending me signals.
I now realize, being a minimizer
is lethal and just plain stupid.

Second Chances

I have always believed
in the redemption
of second chances,
the opportunity to change,
to forgive one's past flaws,
a chance to free oneself
from the burdensome steel boots
of resistance,
a moment to discover
psychic energy and strength
in my best choices.
There is that moment
you realize knowledge is power,
it is possible to align
health and spirit,
intellect and energy.
I accept the brutal truth,
my parts will eventually
wear out,
But I must respect
my body's strength
to restore itself
and not allow
any of my parts
to rust before
their time.

**This poem was inspired by my mother, who famously said, "We are like cars. Our parts will eventually wear out."*

Rehab Buddies

A routine, a ritual, it is healing
after a life-altering event.
Camaraderie ensues quickly
in the cardiac rehabilitation room.
We are there to keep the blood pumping
to our hearts, to test our surgeries,
to keep moving in spite of our setbacks.
I am talking to a retired newspaper photographer.
We share fond memories of working
in a newsroom for many years.
Another man wears Bible verses on his T-shirt.
He and I have an unexpectedly respectful
conversation about salvation and the afterlife,
a way more interesting way to pass the time
than staring out the window
at the hospital parking lot.
Another man has interesting tattoos
and looks way too young and way too buffed
to have had a heart attack.
We are both foodies, always looking for ways
to re-negotiate our relationship with food.
We both struggle with the eternal question,
how do we avoid salt
when we like going to restaurants?
A sweet widow projects great determination
to overcome all obstacles
life has thrown her way.
A community of survivors working our tails off
to stay alive.
We know we are in it to win it.

Our perceived differences disappear
in the comfort of our rituals,
in the urgency of our health goals.
Without the gang, our three-times-a-week
rehab would feel like drudgery,
a drawn-out prison sentence for the afflicted.
Instead, it feels like a summer camp with friends,
an exclamation mark to shout,
we made it together,
and we reached our heart goals
with joy and purpose.

An Integrated Life

Mind, body, and spirit,
that is the truest,
most sacred path.
I always cultivated
my intellect, but
I ignored my body,
the importance of
physical energy,
the essence of
staying strong.
The spirit guides all.
Call it faith,
a belief in legacy,
a joy in purpose,
a sense of my place
in the universe.
I neglected to water
the entire garden
with knowledge,
awareness, and spirit.
All paths intersect.
I had to learn that
the hard way.
To find joy
and purpose
in my life
is the only way
to blossom.
I believe we were

meant to blossom,
not merely survive.
Body, mind, and spirit,
I am finding my way
to an integrated life.

We Need Poets

A friend told me
he is glad
I am alive.
In the tidal wave
of political unrest,
he reminded me
we need poets to be
the steady North Stars.
That was one
of the nicest things
anyone told me
after the heart attack.
The vitality
of my brain,
the emotional depth
of my spirit,
those just might be
my survival tools.
In the midst of
heart failure,
I needed to know
I still have the strength
and stamina
to move people
with my words.
It is a gift
I will not squander.

A Loud Alarm Clock

I hate when people say
the heart attack
was a wake-up call.
That's like saying
an earthquake,
a nuclear blast,
or a cat making love
under your bedroom window
are great alarm clocks.
NOT!

Again

Once I recovered
from the heart attack,
and I understood
the gravity of what
happened,
my life suddenly
became divided
into two chapters —
before the heart attack
and after the heart attack.
Life in retirement
was supposed to be
a smooth transition,
without major disruptions.
A heart attack
was never planned
or anticipated.
The surgeons mended
my heart with stents.
In my logical brain,
I knew if I did
all the right things,
my arteries would
continue to pump
blood to all four
chambers of my heart.
The picture of my

heart even proved
I am on the right track.
Logic is a powerful
tool, but the emotions
of my heart attack
made me wonder,
what if it happens again?
What if I am not so lucky
next time?
What if I am driving a car,
and I veer off the road?
Worse, what if I kill others
having a coronary?
So many what if's
never before imagined.
Rational thinking
occasionally feels
like a shaky proposition.
The Silent Killer,
will it strike again?
I can't say, but all
I can do is live a full
life, make healthy
decisions, and try my best
not to give in to the fear
of what might happen
in this less-than-predictable life.
Maybe a little chunk of my soul
died when my heart failed.
But having a clean start
gave me faith that it will be alright.

We all have to
leave this world sometime.
But my emotions in the
deepest core of my heart
tell me, it will not be
any day soon.

Daily Comforts

This coffee,
creamed and sugared
just the way I like it,
a cat on my side
extends his paws
in love and trust,
his sparkling green eyes
beam meadows of comfort,
he stretches closer,
all fur and warmth,
I only feel the crush
of his gentle purrs.

Changes

I used to be
butter obsessed.
I put butter
on everything,
even frozen
dinners.
I used to
eat an entire
bagel.
I used to
consume
too many
sugary snacks.
I am still
a foodie,
but I am
enjoying more
healthy foods,
exercising
portion control,
seeking energy
in the foods
I choose.
Not giving
up on flavors,
textures,
or the foods
I crave.
I slice apples

all day.
I eat hummus
and Greek yogurt
every morning.
I am obsessed
with perfectly
ripe avocadoes.
I eat two squares
of dark chocolate
almost every day.
Hard to believe
there is a chocolate
that is good
for your heart.
I realize I have
a second chance.
Not everyone
has that luxury.
This time I plan
to get it right.

Heart Patient RX

The heart chakra,
such a powerful, fiery source.
Embrace its flaming energy.
Listen to its beautiful,
steady rhythms.
Grasp its power, its strength.
Always honor this sacred life
your heart allows you to live.
Restore.
Refresh.
Revitalize.
Always keep moving.

**A chakra is an energy source in the body. It is a spiritual, not a medical term.*

Survivor

I am more than
just the sum of
my symptoms,
the severity of
my blockages,
the trauma of
my heart attack.
In the old days,
if you had a heart
attack, you died,
or you lost
your zest for life.
Now the worn-out
arteries have new life.
I know I am
a heart patient.
That does not begin
to describe me.
I am a heart attack
survivor.
I hope one day
to be a heart attack
thriver.

Truth Time

"Is your cardiac rehab almost over?"
a friend innocently asked me.
"Not really," I responded.
"It doesn't work that way."
12 weeks of exercise is just a start.
A graduation certificate
will not complete my journey.
I will continue my work-outs
until I stop breathing.
We heart patients have to
work extra hard to maintain
our cardiac health.
It is a life-time commitment.
The pay-off is, I get to live.

My New Mantra

Faith over religiosity.
Gratitude over bitterness.
Resolve over despair.
Acceptance over resistance.
Prayer over powerlessness.
Energy over debilitation.
Trust in the miracle of medicine.
Faith in my own healing.
Belief in my soul and spirit.

Testaments of Our Lives

Body image and health
always felt like
compartmentalized notions.
Now I want to merge
the dance of sensuality
with the comfort
of understanding
the nuances of my body,
finally accepting
that each dark line
and skin crease,
every battle scar
and bruise, are the
rugged rewards of
embracing a robust,
invigorating life.
The realization,
our bodies are
the road maps
of our imperfect lives,
demonstrates why
the trip is fraught
with detours,
interruptions,
unpredictability.
With time and distance,
we can finally grasp,
perfection is not
true beauty.

The Sweetest

Some of the lessons
we learn later in life
are the sweetest.

Gracefully and gratefully, poet Terry Loncaric reflects upon her personal journey through the all-too-common life-altering event of a heart attack with wit, introspection, and clear-headed honesty. Her book of poems, *On the Other Side of a Heart Attack,* examines the fears and emotions of teetering so close to death. With sly humor, Loncaric finds gratitude in surviving her medical emergency, joy in her "rehab buddies," nostalgia in her loving relationship with butter, and a deep determination to avoid the next "big one." Readers needn't be heart attack survivors to appreciate this thoughtful volume. They need only to be human.

Mark Taylor, journalist, author, and heart attack survivor

Terry's poetry offers a raw and truly heartfelt glimpse into the emotional landscape of recovery, capturing both vulnerability and resilience after suffering a heart attack. Her poems beautifully capture the emotional highs and lows of her journey in a way that feels both honest and uplifting.

Karthik Challa, MD, interventional cardiologist

On the Other Side of a Heart Attack is a profoundly moving and impactful read. I was deeply impressed by Terry's ability to transform her intensely personal journey of surviving a heart attack into powerful poetry. The book meticulously guides the reader through the "fragile, emotional, vulnerable, and reflective" experience of a heart attack, detailing the day-by-day progression and the arduous recovery process that accompanies it. The "raw poetry" is particularly lauded, serving as a catalyst for healing, rebuilding, and strength.

Beyond the individual experience, I especially appreciated "Rehab Buddies" which thoughtfully explores the lives of others navigating similar life-altering events, underscoring the universal nature of recovery. As Terry points out in "Truth Time," true engagement with life after such an event is not a fleeting moment but "a lifetime commitment."

Rebecca Fox, RN, BSN

www.ingramcontent.com/pod-product-compliance
Ingram Content Group UK Ltd.
Pitfield, Milton Keynes, MK11 3LW, UK
UKHW041317190726
13845UKWH00025B/323

9 789363 545151